GALE

CENGAGE Learning

Drama for Students, Volume 3

Staff

Editorial: David M. Galens, *Editor.* Terry Browne, Christopher Busiel, Clare Cross, Tom Faulkner, John Fiero, David M. Galens, Carole Hamilton, Sheri Metzger, Daniel Moran, Terry Nienhuis, William P. Wiles, Joanne Woolway, Etta Worthington, *Entry Writers.* Elizabeth Cranston, Kathleen J. Edgar, Jennifer Gariepy, Dwayne D. Hayes, Kurt Kuban, Joshua Kondek, Tom Ligotti, Scot Peacock, Patti Tippett, Pam Zuber, *Contributing Editors.* James Draper, *Managing Editor.* Diane Telgen, *"For Students" Line Coordinator.* Jeffery Chapman, *Programmer/Analyst.*

Research: Victoria B. Cariappa, *Research Team Manager.* Andy Malonis, Barb McNeil, *Research Specialists.* Julia C. Daniel, Tamara C. Nott, Tracie A. Richardson, Cheryl L. Warnock, *Research Associates.* Phyllis P. Blackman, Jeffrey D. Daniels,

Corrine A. Stocker, *Research Assistants*.

Permissions: Susan M. Trosky, *Permissions Manager*. Kimberly F. Smilay, *Permissions Specialist*. Steve Cusack and Kelly A. Quin, *Permissions Associates*.

Production: Mary Beth Trimper, *Production Director*. Evi Seoud, *Assistant Production Manager*. Shanna Heilveil, *Production Assistant*.

Graphic Services: Randy Bassett, *Image Database Supervisor*. Robert Duncan and Michael Logusz, *Imaging Specialists*. Pamela A. Reed, *Photography Coordinator*. Gary Leach, *Macintosh Artist*.

Product Design: Cynthia Baldwin, *Product Design Manager*. Cover Design: Michelle DiMercurio, *Art Director*. Page Design: Pamela A. E. Galbreath, *Senior Art Director*.

editors or publisher. Errors brought to the attention of the publisher and verified to the satisfaction of the publisher will be corrected in future editions.

This publication is a creative work fully protected by all applicable copyright laws, as well as by misappropriation, trade secret, unfair competition, and other applicable laws. The authors and editors of this work have added value to the underlying factual material herein through one or more of the following: unique and original selection, coordination, expression, arrangement, and classification of information. All rights to this publication will be vigorously defended.

Copyright © 1998
Gale Research
835 Penobscot Building
645 Griswold
Detroit, MI 48226-4094

This book is printed on acid-free paper that meets the minimum requirements of American National Standard for Information Sciences—Permanence Paper for Printed Library Materials, ANSI Z39.48-1984.

ISBN 0-7876-2752-6
ISSN 1094-9232
Printed in the United States of America

10 9 8 7 6 5 4 3 2

"Master Harold". . . and the Boys

Athol Fugard 1982

Introduction

First produced at the Yale Repertory Theater in 1982, Athol Fugard's *"Master Harold"* . . . *and the Boys* is based on the playwright's early life in South Africa. But the play itself is not a simple retelling of an incident from his past. Rather, Fugard has presented a personal experience that extends to universal humanity. If the play were simply a polemic against the policy of apartheid, it would already be outdated now that sweeping change has transformed South Africa. Instead, Fugard wrote a play about human relationships that are put to the test by societal and personal forces.

Because Fugard (critically) focused most of his work on the injustices of the apartheid system of South Africa's government, government officials called many of Fugard's works subversive and several times attempted to prevent publication and/or production of his plays. Much of his early work was presented to small private audiences to avoid government censorship. "*Master Harold*" . . . *and the Boys*, however, played 344 performances on Broadway and was produced in other major cities including London. The play was officially banned by the South African government. Despite the efforts of his native country, the wider world community did not ignore Fugard's work and "*Master Harold*" . . . *and the Boys* earned the Drama Desk Award and Critics Circle Award for best play in 1983, and London's *Evening Standard* Award in 1984. The play has subsequently earned a place in contemporary world drama, enjoying frequent revivals around the world. It is considered to be one of Fugard's masterpieces and a vital work valued for both its universal themes of humanity and its skilled theater craft.

Author Biography

Harold Athol Fugard was born June 11, 1932, in Middleburg, Cape Province, South Africa (and later raised in Port Elizabeth, South Africa), to a father who was English and a mother who was Afrikaner (a white South African descended from Dutch settlers). Fugard described his father as a man "full of pointless, unthought-out prejudices." His mother, on the other hand, felt "outrage and anger over the injustice of [South African] society"—particularly the system of apartheid that established separate, unequal rights for whites and blacks.

Fugard attended Port Elizabeth Technical College and the University of Cape Town, where he studied philosophy. He dropped out in 1953, just prior to graduation, however, and toured the world as a crew member of a tramp steamer bound from the Sudan to the Far East between 1953 and 1955. During this time he attempted to write a novel but, dissatisfied with what he produced, he destroyed the manuscript. A few years later, just about the time of his marriage to South African actress Sheila Meiring in 1956, Fugard developed an interest in writing for the stage.

His first full length plays, *No-Good Friday* (1956) and *Nongogo* (1957) grew out of his experiences in Johannesburg, South Africa, in the late 1950s. Fugard worked there briefly as a clerk in the Native Commissioner's Court, which tried cases against nonwhites (the South African term for black citizens) who had been arrested for failing to carry identification. "I knew the system was evil," Fugard recalled, "but until then I had no idea of just how systematically evil it was. That was my revelation." These initial plays were performed by Fugard and black amateur actors for small private audiences.

After a brief move to England in 1959, Fugard returned to South Africa and completed a novel, *Tsotsi*. Although he attempted to destroy this manuscript as he had an earlier one, a copy survived and was published twenty years later. Fugard's first major theatrical success was *The Blood Knot* (1961), a story about the sense of conflict and harmony between two non white half-brothers. First presented to a private audience in 1961, the play featured Fugard as the light-skinned brother, Morris, and actor Zakes Mokae—who became a close friend and long time Fugard collaborator—as the dark-skinned brother, Zach. In *The Blood Knot*, Fugard dramatizes the racial hatred that infects so many South African relationships. This ambivalence perverts the "blood knot," or common bond of humanity.

In 1983, Fugard earned the Drama Desk Award and the Critic's Circle Award for best play and, in 1984, the *Evening Standard* of London award for *"Master Harold". . . and the Boys*. Widely considered Fugard's best and most autobiographical play, *"Master Harold"* centers on the relationship of two black waiters, Sam and Willy, to Hally ("Master Harold"), a white teenager embittered by the neglect of his alcoholic, racist father.

In addition to his plays and notebooks, Fugard has also written screenplays for *Boseman and Lena* (based on his play), 1972; *The Guest*, 1976; *Meetings with Remarkable Men*, 1979; *Marigolds in August*, 1980; *Ghandi*, 1982; and *The Killing Fields*, 1984.

Plot Summary

"*Master Harold*" . . . *and the Boys* is a one-act that takes place inside the St. George's Park Tea Room on a wet and windy Port Elizabeth (South Africa) afternoon in 1950. No customers populate the restaurant and most of tables and chairs have been stacked to one side. Two black waiters, Willie and Sam, are on stage as the play begins. Willie is mopping the floor, and Sam is reading comic books at a table which has been set for a meal. Willie wants to improve his dancing skills but appears to have been deserted by his partner after he beat her. Sam offers Willie advice about improving both his dancing technique and his domestic relations.

The son of the tea room's owner, Hally, enters direct from school. He eats a bowl of soup and talks to the two men with whom he appears to have a close relationship. Hally, while displaying obvious affection for the men—especially Sam—takes a pedantic tone, assuming the role of teacher. Yet the nature of their interaction clearly shows Sam as the teacher and Hally as the eager pupil. Their discussion ranges from what Hally has been learning at school about great men of history to reminiscences of the old Jubilee Boarding House, where the young Hally used to hide in Sam and Willie's room. They also talk about the kite that Sam made for Hally and taught him how to fly as well as the art of ballroom dancing.

The recollection of the kite has special significance for Sam and Hally. The kite is a symbol of their deep friendship. An incident from a few years prior is recalled in which Sam had to carry Hally's father, drunken to the point of incoherence, home. The boy was deeply ashamed of his father and greatly depressed by the incident. Sam built him the kite as a symbol of their friendship and to give Hally something to which he could, figuratively and literally, look up, holding his head high ("I wanted you to look up, be proud of something, of yourself. . .").

From the exchanges between Hally and the two men and two one-sided telephone conversations, it becomes apparent that Hally's crippled and drunken father is to return home from the hospital that day. Hally loves his father but is also ashamed of him and wants him to remain at the hospital. At first the boy pretends that it isn't true, that his father will remain at the hospital indefinitely, preserving the idyllic quality of Hally's recent life. Yet as the realization sinks in, Hally becomes depressed and tells Sam that it might be time to build another kite.

As his father's return becomes imminent, Hally's mood changes drastically. He becomes brutally rude to the two men, insults them with racial slurs, and, in an act of cruel insolence, spits in Sam's face. Sam starts forward as if he means to strike the boy, but Willie restrains him. Sam regains his composure and, removing his white servant's jacket, extends his hand to Hally in a gesture of equality, friendship, and forgiveness. The boy, however, is too ashamed of his cruelty to even look the older man in the face. Hally departs, and Sam and Willie dance together as Sarah Vaughn sings the blues.

Hally

Seventeen-year old Hally, the white son of the owners of the St. George's Park Tea Room, is the "Master Harold" of the title. Hally appears devoted to Sam, one of two black waiters employed by his family's business. The young man takes great pride in "educating" Sam through brief recapitulations of lessons learned from books and in the classroom. But, in reality, it has been Sam who has been "educating" the young man, teaching him the ways of the world. Hally, however, has been affected by both the South African apartheid society of the late 1950s, which has taught him to view nonwhites as second-class citizens, and his drunken father's inability to serve as a parent. When Hally learns that his father is coming home from the alcoholic ward of the local hospital, he is conflicted with feelings of both love and shame. The self-assured young man of the beginning of the play degenerates into an embittered child who lashes out at the nearest target —Sam. At the play's conclusion, the student who had all the answers for his "pupil" leaves the tea room confused and in pain.

Media Adaptations

- *"Master Harold"*. . . *and the Boys* was adapted as a television film in 1985. Produced by Lorimar pictures and directed by Michael Lindsay-Hogg, this production starred Matthew Broderick as Hally, John Kani as Willie, and longtime Fugard collaborator Zakes Mokae as Sam. It is available on video through Facets Video.

Fugard himself served as the model for Hally. As he recalled in a 1961 entry in his memoir *Notebooks*, the man whose full name is Harold Athol Lannigan Fugard (he was called Hally as a youth) was ashamed of his father, a lame man with a drinking problem. But, Fugard did not simply retell what happened in his life, choosing instead to embellish and slightly alter the story. For instance, Fugard was fourteen at the time of the play's pivotal episode, but he makes his character Hally three years older. Additionally, the incident where Hally spits in Sam's face did not take place in the cafe but while Hally (Fugard) was bicycling. In the same entry dated March, 1961, Fugard vaguely "recall[s] shyly haunting the servants' quarters in the well of the hotel. . . a world [he] didn't fully understand."

He refers in this entry to Sam as "the most significant, the only friend of [his] boyhood years."

Master Harold

See Hally

Sam

Sam, a black man in his mid-forties, is a waiter at the St. George Park Tea Room owned by Hally's parents. He has been employed by the family a long time, at least since the days of the Jubilee Boarding House. He has served as a father figure to young Hally while the boy's father spends time in and out of the hospital recovering from bouts of alcoholism. After one particularly humiliating episode for Hally, where Sam carried the boy's drunken father home on his back, Sam made a kite for Hally out of brown paper and tomato-box wood with water and flour for glue. He built the kite because he wanted Hally to "look up, be proud of something." When Hally, in frustration and rage at things beyond his control, spits in his face, Sam offers his young friend a chance at reconciliation. An offer that is refused by Hally.

Not just a servant, Sam is a recognized expert, at least by Willie and Hally, on dance. He offers advice to both his fellow waiter, Willie, as well as Hally on the intricacies and symbolic nature of ballroom dancing. "There's no collisions out there, Hally. Nobody trips or stumbles or bumps into anybody else. That's what the moment is all about. To be one of those finalists on that dance floor is like . . . like being in a dream about a world in which accidents don't happen . . . it's beautiful because that is what we want life to be like."

The character of Sam is based on Sam Semela, a Basuto (a tribe of people who live in the Lesotho region of South Africa) who worked for Fugard's family for fifteen years. Fugard's mother fired Sam when he became careless and began arriving late for work. Fugard remembers his mother saying, "His work went to hell. He didn't seem to care no more."

Willie

Willie also works at the St. George Tea Room as a waiter. Much of his attention is centered on the upcoming ballroom dancing championships. He takes much good-natured ribbing from Sam about practicing his dancing with a pillow. When Hally arrives, Willie assumes the servant role, referring to Hally as "Master Harold." Throughout much of the play, Willie observes, but rarely comments on, the exchanges between Sam and Hally. In the pivotal scene where Hally spits in Sam's face, it is Willie who groans ("long and heartfelt" according to the stage directions); it is Willie who stops Sam from hitting Hally; it is Willie who says that if Hally had spit in his face, he would also want to hit him hard, but would probably just go cry in the back room. Ultimately, Willie crystallizes the emotion of the play: "Is bad. Is all bad in here now."

Themes

Anger and Hatred

"*Master Harold*" . . . *and the Boys* presents in vivid detail what happens in a society constructed in institutional anger and hatred (apartheid). The policies of the South African government in the mid-1950s legislated a certain amount of hatred and anger between whites and blacks. Sam, long a victim of these official and traditional policies, has attempted to transcend the hatred and anger. He acts as a surrogate father to Hally, fortifying the boy's sense of well-being (both through kind acts such as building the kite and through allowing the boy to teach him what he learned in school) and imparting his wisdom to Hally in a series of life lessons (his dance hall metaphors for peaceful coexistence). That a seventeen-year-old can spit in the face of a black man without even the thought of repercussions shines a harsh light onto the institutional policies of hatred that were fostered in South Africa.

Hally must also cope with his own feelings of anger and hatred toward his father, feelings that are conflicted by his simultaneous love for his father. After each of the telephone calls, Hally becomes dark and sullen. The humanitarian affirmations he had been espousing prior to the phone calls evaporate into confusion and anger. Even though

Sam is the recipient of the most vicious insult, it is his father who is the true focal point of Hally's rage. Societal taboos and restrictions prevent Hally from telling his father what he really thinks. Those same societal influences allow Hally to redirect his anger and frustration to Sam without fear of consequences. The aftermath, however, is far more destructive than any punishment, as Hally must carry with him the knowledge that he has gravely wronged one of his truest friends.

Human Rights

The South African system of apartheid comes under heavy attack in "*Master Harold*" . . . *and the Boys* despite the fact that apartheid is not directly addressed in the play. Instead, it is the society that the system has created that is criticized. It is not merely that racial prejudice is legislated in South Africa. This prejudice weasels its way into every facet of life, so much so that the language begins to reflect the disparity of power where black men are forced by law to be subservient to white children. The young Hally with the appropriately immature nickname transforms into "Master Harold" in the context of the prejudicial attitudes promoted by apartheid. On the other hand, Sam, the white boy's mentor and surrogate father, is regarded as the "boy," a second-class citizen who is looked down upon. Yet Sam's maturity and honor are clearly shown in his compassion, humanity, and sense of what is right and wrong.

Within the culture of the play, there is nothing unusual about a white child hitting or degrading a black man. It would have been unheard of for the black man in the South Africa of the 1950s to strike back, however. His anger and frustration could only be released on those even more dispossessed: black women and children. The white child hits the black man, the black man hits the black woman, the black woman hits the black child. It is a system in which violence spirals downward in a hierarchy of degradation, as evidenced in Willie's abusive relationship with his dancing partner.

Rites of Passage

Hally has two courses of action open to him in his journey toward maturity—the loving, reasoned way of Sam or the indifferent, humiliating way of Hally's father and the rest of South African society. Sam offers Hally more than one opportunity to break with institutional forms of racism and embark on a new course. Sam is tempted to strike back after Hally spits in his face but, instead, tries to turn the occasion into a positive learning experience that will guide the boy towards better relationships with his fellow man.

For Sam, the appropriate action is in virtue rather than violence, in reasoning rather than rage. Sam trusts in his capacity to move Hally to shame through exemplary behavior and an appeal to morality. He forgives the white boy who doesn't know any better and behaves like a "man" in order to teach Hally the basics of honorable behavior. In a challenge to change what has happened through an act of personal transformation, Sam extends his hand toward Hally in a gesture of reconciliation. "You don't *have* to sit up there by yourself," he says, recalling Hally's feeling of isolation on the "Whites Only" bench. "You know what that bench means now and you can leave it any time you choose. All you've got to do is stand up and walk away from it." The invitation to "walk away" is a chance to leave Hally's past behind, to abandon the ways of apartheid and become an honorable adult. Hally, however, is paralyzed by both shame and the ingrained attitudes fostered by society; he cannot break free of them to begin his journey as a "man."

Topics for Further Study

- Research the South African system of apartheid. Compare that system to the segregated system of "separate but equal" that existed in the United States in the 1950s. What differences in the respective governments of the two countries enabled the U.S. to overcome racial inequalities before South Africa?

- Discuss the episode of the kite, particularly in the light of Sam's explanation after Hally has spit in his face.

- Sam discusses the complexities of human relations by using the metaphor of dance. Show how this metaphor works in the context of the play.

- Hally has two one-sided telephone conversations during the play. Discuss his mood after each one. Why is the second call more troubling than the first?

- Almost all of the dialogue in the play is between Sam and Hally. What is Willie's role in this drama? Is it mere observer? Or is his role more significant than that?

Style

Setting

"*Master Harold*" . . . *and the Boys* is a drama set in the St. George's Tea Room on a wet and windy afternoon. The year is 1950 and the location is Port Elizabeth, South Africa. The entire play takes place in the restaurant. While it is a small, enclosed space, the tea room serves as a microcosm of South African society at large. The attitudes and situations that are displayed in the restaurant are variations on what occurred on a daily basis under the system of apartheid.

Realism

"*Master Harold*" . . . *and the Boys* subscribes to the school of realism in that the actions and dialogue of the three characters are very much as they would be in real life. This is not surprising given that the play is based on events from Fugard's own life. Like his titular character, the playwright had the nickname Hally as well as an alcoholic father of whom he was greatly ashamed. Fugard found a surrogate father in a black man who worked at his parents' cafe, a relationship much like the one between Hally and Sam. The play also enacts a historical reality in its portrayal of the actions and attitudes of South Africa at the height of apartheid.

Yet realism in literature is not a mere transcription of actual events; it seeks to use reality as a kind of mirror in which the audience can see themselves. Fugard uses realistic events and settings to strike chords of recognition in his audience. The play may be based on a specific event from his own childhood, but the themes of societal prejudice are universal. By portraying the severe emotional toll that is exacted when inequality is a fundamental concept in society, the playwright hopes to make his viewers aware and hopefully prevent future instances of injustice. The play is not about the history of apartheid politics but more specifically a family history that illustrates the evils of such a prejudiced system.

Symbolism

Two images play prominent roles in this drama: the kite and dancing. Made out of tomato-box slats, brown paper, discarded socks, and glue, the kite represents the soaring hopes for equality between the races and the triumph of human love over prejudice and hatred. Sam made the kite for Hally to lift the boy's spirits. A past incident is recalled in which Hally's father had become so drunk at a local bar that he had soiled himself. Because the mother was not at home, Hally had to go to the bar and ask permission for Sam to enter in order to take his father home. The event greatly disturbed and depressed the boy. Sam tells Hally he made the kite because he "wanted [him] to look up, be proud of something, of [him]self." At the end of the play, after Hally has spit in his face, Sam, in a final attempt at reconciliation, offers Hally the opportunity to "fly another kite." "You can't fly kites on rainy days," says Hally. This exchange illustrates the two characters' personalities and is also reflective of South African culture at large. Sam, like many South Africans, wishes to reconcile, put the past behind him, and work towards a better future. Hally, also like many of his countrymen, realizes what he has done is wrong yet is too programmed to attempt change.

Dancing assumes the role as metaphor for life in the play. From the tribulations of Willie and his partner to Willie and Sam's poignant dance that concludes the play, dancing helps the characters makes sense of a world that seems out of control. Describing his idea of a perfect ballroom—metaphorically an ideal world—Sam tell Hally, "There are no collisions out there. . . . Nobody trips or stumbles or bumps into anybody else . . . like being in a dream about a world in which accidents don't happen."

Separate and Unequal

In the mid-twentieth century, the country of South Africa was dominated by the policy of apartheid, a separation and segregation based on race. Strict policies prohibited and governed such issues as intermarriage, land ownership, and use of public facilities. In *"Master Harold" . . . and the Boys*, Sam illustrates the division quite clearly: "I couldn't sit down there and stay with you," referring to a "Whites Only" bench upon which Hally sat. The laws deliberately set out to humiliate people of color, even to the point of determining who could sit on a particular bench. Errol Durbach explained the psychopathology of apartheid in *Modern Drama:* "It is not that racial prejudice is *legislated* in South Africa. It insinuates itself into every social sphere of existence, until the very language of ordinary human discourse begins to reflect the policy that makes black men subservient to the power exercised by white children."

Fugard's Underground Theater

Many of Fugard's early plays were performed for small private audiences rather than in public theaters; apartheid laws forbade white actors appearing on stage with black actors. In the 1960s, Fugard helped to start the Serpent Players, an all-black theater group made up of residents of New Brighton, the black township of Fugard's hometown of Port Elizabeth. Despite frequent harassment from the police, the Serpent Players continued to perform, and Fugard's involvement with the group did much to establish black South African theater.

In Fugard's first major theatrical success, *The Blood Knot*, Fugard appeared as a light-skinned nonwhite half brother, a commentary on a individual's search for freedom in a country that denied such independence. In this play, Fugard dramatized the ambivalence and racial hatred that infected many South African relationships, perverting the "blood knot," or common bond of humanity. Despite voicing the concerns of the country's black majority, Fugard's drama was considered rebellious by the white ruling minority. Because it so implicitly criticized the way of life for many Afrikaners, his work was often banned or heavily censored. It was not until "*Master Harold*" . . . *and the Boys*, which had its debut outside of South Africa, that the rest of the world became aware of Fugard's work. With endorsements from critics and audiences in New York and London, "*Master Harold*"'s message was being heard, despite a South African ruling banning performance or publication of the play.

The End of Apartheid

The culture of racism that was promoted by apartheid continued virtually unchecked throughout the 1950s and well into the next three decades. By 1982, apartheid was recognized in much of the free world as a dire injustice against humanity. Activist organizations such as Amnesty International fought for the eradication of such an inherently racist society, going to great lengths to publicize South Africa's criminal treatment of its black majority. Along with the human rights violations of communist China, South Africa's policies were considered among the gravest.

Compare & Contrast

- **1950s:** In South Africa, the system of apartheid legislates the separation of the races. Black people are forced to live in designated areas and may only use designated public facilities.
  1980s: The world condemns the policy of apartheid. Many people across the globe protest the involvement of businesses in South Africa and demonstrate for divestiture of investments in that country.
  Today: The government of South Africa has officially renounced the policy of apartheid and has elected a black leader, Nelson Mandela.

- **1950s:** In America, pre-World War II race restrictions (Jim Crow laws) are discarded. Black people assert their civil rights with marches, demonstrations, sit-down strikes, and boycotts. The Supreme Court strikes down the doctrine of "separate but equal" in the landmark *Brown v. the Board of Education* decision. In the ensuing decade, the Civil Rights Movement will reach a fever pitch, creating sweeping legislation to promote equality among races.

1980s: While race relations in the U.S. have improved since the 1950s and 1960s, there is still considerable inequality to be addressed. These disparities are trivial compared with the plight of South African blacks, however. Expanding public knowledge of apartheid renews many Americans commitment to racial harmony and equality in their own country.

Today: The U.S. has instituted policies that forbid discrimination based on race or color in the areas of employment, housing, and access to government services. Despite the obvious benefits of such policies, many conservative politicians seek to eradicate such practices as Affirmative Action, claiming that it denies qualified whites equal opportunity.

Blacks who spoke out against the government's policies were routinely arrested and imprisoned. The most famous activist/prisoner in the South African penal system was Nelson Mandela, whose public campaigns for equality resulted in a sentence of life imprisonment. At the time of "*Master Harold*"'s, first production in 1982, Mandela was one of the best-known political prisoners in the world. Despite the efforts of the South African government, Mandela's message was being heard across continents. In 1987, while still a prisoner, he was awarded the Nobel Peace Prize. In 1990, then president F. W. de Klerk ordered Mandela's release, after twenty-seven years of incarceration. Soon after, de Klerk dissolved the system of apartheid and agreed to open elections that would allow blacks to both run for office and freely vote. In 1991, Mandela was elected the president of South Africa and his party, the African National Congress, took control of the government. After decades of subordination, South Africa's black majority finally had an equal voice in their country.

Critical Overview

The summary of *"Master Harold"*'s action cannot begin to suggest its emotional intensity or its impact on an audience. Many who saw the play in its debut were greatly troubled by the society it depicted. Since that time *"Master Harold"* has continued to provoke critics and audiences alike.

Errol Durbach, writing in *Modern Drama*, asserted that *"Master Harold". . . and the Boys* is not an overtly political play, but a depiction of "a personal power-struggle with political implications." The only definition that the South African system can conceive of in the relationship of White to Black is one that humiliates black people. This definition "insinuates itself into every social sphere of existence, until the very language of ordinary human discourse begins to reflect the policy that makes black men subservient to the power exercised by white children." In the society depicted by Fugard White equals "Master" and Black equals "boy." It is an equation, continued Durbach, that ignores the traditional relationship of labor to management or of paid employee to paying employer.

During the course of the drama, Hally rapidly realigns the components of his long-standing friendship with Sam into the socio-political patterns of master and servant. Hally changes from intimate familiarity with his black companions to patronizing condescension to his social inferiors. It is an exercise of power by Hally, himself a "boy" who feels powerless to control the circumstance of his life and therefore seeks some measure of autonomy in his interaction with Sam and Willie.

Robert Brustein, in a review in the *New Republic*, described "*Master Harold*" . . . *and the Boys* as the "quintessential racial anecdote," and ascribed to Fugard's writing "a sweetness and sanctity that more than compensates for what might be prosaic, rhetorical, or contrived about it." There is a suggestion that Fugard's obsession with the theme of racial injustice may be an expression of his own guilt and act of expiation. As Brian Crow noted in the *International Dictionary of Theatre*, "biographical information, however, is not needed in order for the play to make its full impact in the theatre. This is achieved primarily through an audience's empathy with the loving relationship between Hally and Sam and its violation through Hally's inability to cope with his emotional turmoil over his father, and its expression in racism. If to what extent the play manages. . . to transmute autobiographical experience into a larger exploration or analysis of racism in South Africa is arguable; what seems quite certain is its capacity to involve and disturb audiences everywhere."

Yet not all critical reaction to Fugard's work has been positive. Failing to see the play's wider message on racism, Stephen Gray saw "*Master Harold*" as nothing more than a play about apartheid. In a 1990 *New Theatre Quarterly* article,

Gray noted that South Africa's dissolution of apartheid has made the play obsolete, stating that it "feels like a museum piece today." Other negative criticism found the play's black characters to be falsely represented. As Jeanne Colleran reported in *Modern Drama*, "To some black critics, the character of Sam is a grotesquerie. His forbearance and forgiveness, far from being virtues, are embodiments of the worst kind of Uncle Tom-ism." Such reproach prompted Fugard to clarify his intentions during the Anson Phelps Stokes Institute's Africa Roundtable. As Colleran reported, Fugard stated that his intention was to tell a story: "I never set out to serve a cause. . . . The question of being a spokesman for Black politics is something I've never claimed for myself."

Such criticism for *"Master Harold"* was sporadic, however. The majority of critics and audiences embraced the play as important and thought-provoking. Commenting on Fugard's ability to fuse theatricality with strong political issues, Dennis Walder wrote in *Athol Fugard*, "Fugard's work. . . contains a potential for subversion, a potential which, I would suggest, is the hallmark of great art, and which qualifies his best work to be called great."

What Do I Read Next?

- *Selected Stories*, a collection of short stories by Nobel-Prize winning author Nadine Gordimer. A white South African like Fugard, Gordimer brings her characters and the African landscape they inhabit to life.

- *Hamlet*, one of William Shakespeare's classic tragedies, was written in approximately 1603. It concerns a young man who has unresolved issues with both his father and his uncle. His inability to articulate his feelings causes him to lash out at people he loves with serious consequences.

- *To Kill a Mockingbird* (1960), a novel by Harper Lee that examines the events of a American town in the South during the Depression. The novel confronts issues of racism and power through the story a black man on trial for the rape of a white woman and the white lawyer who defends him.

- *Black like Me* (1961) a memoir written by John Howard Griffin, recounts the adventures of a white man who changed the pigment of his skin to resemble a black man in the 1950s in the American South. The books offers a unique perspective on the treatment of African Americans during a pivotal time in the history of civil rights.

Sources

Brustein, Robert. Review of "*Master Harold*" in the *New Republic*, Vol. 186, No. 25, June 23, 1982, pp. 30-31.

Colleran, Jeanne. *Modern Drama*, Vol. XXXIII, no. 1, March, 1990, pp. 82-92.

Crow, Brian. "*Master Harold . . . and the Boys*" in *International Dictionary of Theatre*, Vol. 1: *Plays*, edited by Mark Hawkins-Dady, St. James Press, 1992.

Durbach, Errol,"'*Master Harold*' . . . *and the Boys:* Athol Fugard and the Psychopathology of Apartheid" in *Modern Drama*, Vol. XXX, no. 4, December 1987, pp. 505-13.

Gray, Stephen. *New Theatre Quarterly*, Vol. VI, no. 21, February, 1990, pp. 25-30.

Further Reading

Brians, Paul. "Athol Fugard: '*Master Harold*' . . . *and the Boys*" at http://www.wsu.edu:8080/~brians/anglophone/fugar

> A website containing notes to the Penguin Plays edition of "*Master Harold*' . . . *and the Boys* (1984); organized by page number.

Mallaby, Sebastian. *After Apartheid: The Future of South Africa*, Times Books, 1992.

> Polarized by decades of apartheid, black and white South Africans now face the challenges of racial coexistence and economic growth in a new, multiracial nation. This incisive examination of the radical consequences of apartheid's demise offers a penetrating look at South Africa on the brink of racial and historic change.

"Underdog's South African Independent Film Site" at http://www.safilm.org.za/.

> A home page with links to Film Festivals, Film Schools, Showdata's SA Film Site, and other independent South African media artists.

Walder, Dennis. *Athol Fugard*, Macmillan, 1984.

Walder is a South African educator and critic. His book offers analysis of Fugard's career up through 1984 and includes considerable discussion of "*Master Harold.*"

CPSIA information can be obtained
at www.ICGtesting.com
Printed in the USA
BVHW071342140920
588712BV00013B/1130

9 781375 384